The
GOLDEN CHILDREN
of Hawaii

Produced by:
THE MADDEN CORPORATION

Published by:
ISLAND HERITAGE
A Division of The Madden Corporation

Researched and Written by:
RUTH M. TABRAH
ANDERSON BLACK

Art Director:
TED BAPTISTA

Designed by:
THE BAPTISTA GROUP
PAM CASTALDI
Consultant

Photography:
PETER FRENCH
Primary Contributing Photographer

Cover by:
MARY KOSKI
"The Golden Children of Hawaii"
(Original Oil Painting 20" by 42")

*A Special Thanks for the inspiration
provided by the creativity of a
dozen years of "Haku Mele o Hawaii,"
...published by the State of Hawai'i,
Department of Education.*

Please address orders
and editorial correspondence to:
C.H.A.N.G.E.
Davies Pacific Center
841 Bishop Street, Suite 1901
Honolulu, Hawaii 96813

(808) 533-0500

FIRST EDITION—1987

A unique quality of Hawai'i's cosmopolitan mix of peoples is that they live together, work together and play together in an environment of aloha.

The average *ohana*, family group, mingles the heritage of East and West. A child can have ancestors who came from China, Japan, Korea, the South Pacific Islands, like Samoa and Tonga, or the Philippines. Some grandparents may have come from the new countries of North America, the old countries of Europe, or more recently, the countries of Southeast Asia. Many have strands of Polynesian ancestry and all are the golden children of Hawai'i.

They cherish the land of these islands, the *'āina*, and they feel Hawaiian in their hearts. They understand the value of *holoholo*, doing something or nothing in a relaxed way. They know and revere the special celebrations that light their lives. To us, they are very special children on this planet.

This book is for, in part by, and totally about Hawai'i's golden children, whose words and faces tell us so much about how to live in this fragile world. They offer us a poignantly honest, yet brightly shining image of their present. . .and of their and our future.

OHANA

O HANA is the Hawaiian word for family, a network of infinite variety entwining those whose lives are linked through lineage, love, and aloha.

I am a real Hawaiian. I am
part Filipino and Scotch.
I am a girl with long straight hair.
I have brown eyes.
I have plenty of cousins and uncles and
    aunties.
I have many friends.

My family are like dogs and cats
never getting along.
We're all separated like continents
every time we're together.
My mom, my sister and I are like wild
screaming hyenas.
But when we're with our father
My sis and I get along very well
like trees and fruit on the tree stuck
    together.
When the whole family is together we
    are
like rotten fruits on an old ugly tree.
So my family are better off being
    separated
Like the North Pole and the South Pole.

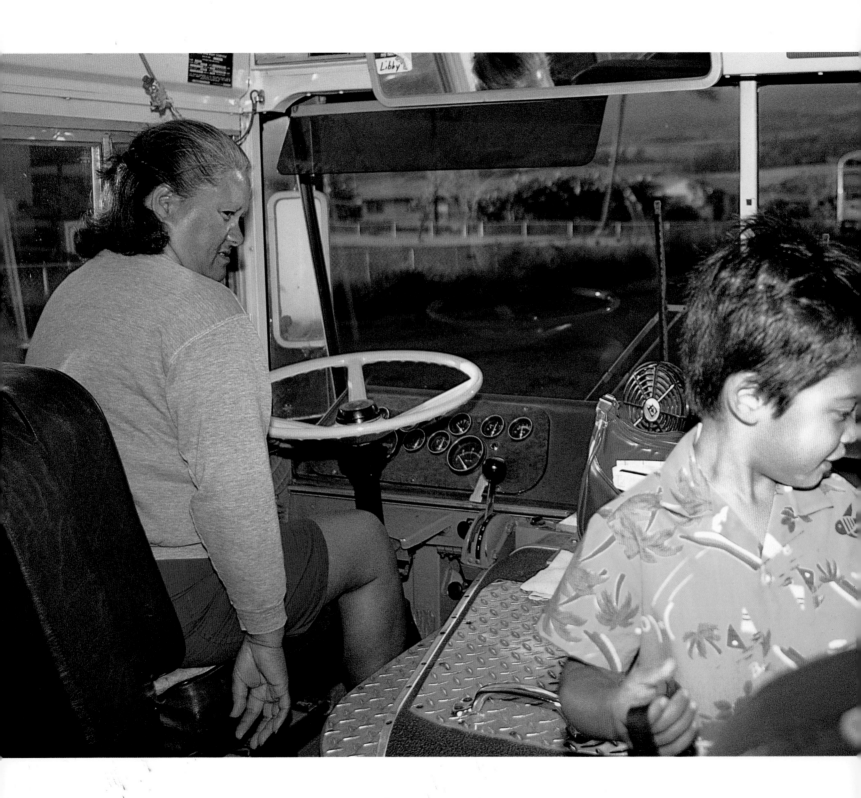

When I look out of my house I see
   banana trees and pigeon peas
So you can tell we are Puerto Ricans.
And also you see some beans and
   cabbages
So someone in our family is a good
   grower.

My mother is driving a school bus.
After she is done she is going to wash
   her hair
and after that she is going to watch a
   sad movie
and she is going to cry.
Then she is going to cook dinner.
She will take a bath and hear the
   sound of water.
And then she will call my father
and tell him to come home.

◀

My father is a commercial fisherman.
We have our own boat.
I went out with my father about a
    month ago.
We came in with 700 lbs. of fish.

▶

Me and my father like to cut wood and
    dive.
When we go diving we catch
Squid and lobster and all kinds of
    fishes.
To catch a lobster is to go in a cave.
And to catch a squid is to look under
    the rocks.

My Daddy had red steam coming out
  of his ears.
He was so angry that the whole house
  turned red.
We couldn't get it off the walls and the
  furniture.
We were tired of living in the house so
  we moved.
When we moved into a new house,
We had Daddy have his ears checked.

Kupuna is the Hawaiian word for grand-
parent. For golden children, a *kupuna* is
very special.

▲
My great grandmother died.
She's in a grave.
Sometimes I pray for her.
She died when I was only four.
We give her flowers and pour water on
    her stone.
At her grave we cry in silence.

▶

A family is a wilderness of nice people.

G olden children cherish the
AINA, the land of these islands
that once upon a time rose like
gifts from the bottom of the sea.
Pele produced them all, as a Hilo
child says:

◀

The rhythm of the volcano
is like a waterfall when it falls to the
   ground,
the chant of a beautiful song.

▶

For an Oahu boy, the clouds pour on
   the mountains like syrup on his
   pancakes.

▲

A boy in rural Oahu thinks
The chain of islands is like
My chain of brothers.
First is me, I'm 9, the oldest,
Then my brother Jason is 8,
And my baby brother is one.

▶

On Lanai there are sunsets that look
    like they have rusted.

▲

On windy days in Oahu's mountains
   the bamboo forests bend as if in prayer.

◀

On my mom's Kohala ranch I can look
out and see forever.

▶

Keanae Maui is quiet and peaceful.
It has waterfalls that run from the
   mountain to the sea.
When I wake up in the morning, I can
   see the clear mountains (sometimes
   cloudy).
I like living in Keanae because you
   don't have to wake up and see all the
   crowded houses and buildings,
And you don't have to listen to the
   sound of traffic
And angry people blowing their horns.
It's just peaceful.

In the forest behind Manoa Valley,
The wind made a path through the
   dirt
So I followed it home.

Behind me, the mountains just sit there
   facing the sky every year.

In the taro patches of Hanalei Valley on
  Kauai there's mud like you have never
  seen before — not even in the city.

There are valleys full of hibiscus on
  Molokai.

A Makawao Maui girl says my
  grandma's farm is like a jungle with
  all the life flowing over it.
There are goats, rabbits, cows, — and
  me, of course.

▲
Kahoolawe is an island with trees
   growing
and birds that fly over it
and people that bomb it.

▶

   Waipio Valley is a very good place to
live. I should know because I live there.
Every day when I come home from
school or I'm just at home, I can see
lots of mountains, trees, grass, dirt.
   We have a farm in Waipio Valley. The
animals I see are horses, dogs, cats,
pigs, cows, rabbits and mice. There are
rivers and streams. We give them
names.
   The flowers smell good here. You can
talk to the trees and flowers. I know it
sounds dumb but when there's nothing
to do that's the thing to do so I do it.

Recipe for an Island

Ingredients: Baking pan, rain
a bowl 2 feet
water "5 miles"
pinch of sand
coconuts
palm trees
a teaspoon of
    loneliness
flower
sunshine

Step I: get the bowl and put
in 5 miles of water.
add the coconuts, mix
and set aside.

Step II: get another bowl, put
in palm trees, sand,
flowers and loneliness.
Mix

Step III: mix all ingredients
together and put in
baking pan

Step IV: put in the rain for 5
minutes and then take
out. Cool and then
sprinkle with
sunshine. Serve
immediately!

An island is all the people we love to be
around.

FEELINGS

Whether their ancestors came from east, west, south or north, the golden children of Hawaii feel Hawaiian at heart. They have a fresh new way of communicating their FEELINGS.

Theirs is the honesty of how things really are. This communication is not always verbal. It says not how we think they ought to be or wish they were but what they think, feel, and are.

Sometimes their candor wounds us. What have we been teaching them for our children to think *that*! But their values, frank and reality-related, show a warmth that can light up the future for us all.

We like to dance our feelings.

Language of our generation
often requires translation
in order to produce communication.

Can
Any
Mother
Be Right
All the time?

There's no limit to where I can climb!

Toes are like fingers that haven't passed
   the test.

Sometimes it takes a boy
Years and years of steady growing
To become big enough to match
   the name
That his parents gave him.

My mind feels like my mother's purse,
always trying to hold more than it can.

As hard as showing your mother your bad grades.

On the last day of school I got on my bike
and burned rubber.

▲

My ears are like radars.
They catch a sound like a fisherman
    catches fish,
Like a frog catches bugs.
If we didn't have ears the world would
    be in silence
and ears can hear somebody say
    I love you.

▶

thinking
a lot
makes me laugh!

Sometimes you think
You don't know anything.
Sometimes you think
You know everything.
Sometimes you think
You know a lot but not enough.
Sometimes you think
It's better not to think!

Even though my thoughts were like
I was going to be a little sad,
I really enjoyed myself yesterday.

Sometimes I wish I was a white dove.
A white dove would remind people of
    love and freedom.
I would fly all around the world
    whispering peace.

It's also peaceful to be all alone in
    a forest.

Me and my dog find peace on the
    beach sometimes.

But sometimes I think life is for
the birds.

According to Mary Kawena Pukui's Hawaiian Dictionary, HOLOHOLO once meant to 'walk about' or 'sail about'. The golden children of modern Hawaii value HOLOHOLO as the art of doing something or doing nothing, in a relaxed way.

◀

Exploring with mask and snorkel

▶

Holoholo can happen any time, any-where.

Fishing on the Ala Wai

Paddling a canoe

One day me and my friends went surfing.
Plenty big the waves!
I was riding a wave, it scared me half
    to death —
Eleven feet is three times as big as me.
That kind of wave I was shredding
And doing some mean cutbacks.
When we came out of the water, tired!
So we headed home.

▲

There are some who prefer to bodysurf.

◀

Windsurfing is great too.

▶

You can just cruise and take in the scenery.

When you want to cool off, it's with
    shave ice,
an *ono* treat for visitors too.

Hanging out with Grandpa

Holoholo can be tuning up the 'bug',

Or catching the train on Maui.

From town to town people buy things, writes a boy who's seen what girls like to do.

Feeding the ducks at Punaluu

▲
In the middle of Honolulu you can
holoholo where it's still like it
used to be.

▶
In the city there are parks to picnic in.

Some days you want to just go fly a kite.

What may look like work for a father can be *holoholo* for a small boy.

Holoholo is also doing nothing with someone special.

SPECIAL

So much of what these golden children do is very SPECIAL. They know and revere the multicultural celebrations that are special to Hawaii. Blessed with rich imaginations, they like to imagine doing — and seeing SPECIAL things, like "being spotted by the moon."

Never did I see a big toad in a
   supermarket
croaking at the cashier
and handing the peanut butter and the
   olives to her
like the one I saw yesterday evening!

One day I followed the rainbow and
   end up lost.

On a night of June I saw some green
   men from the moon
so I put on my armour and said,
   let's talk!

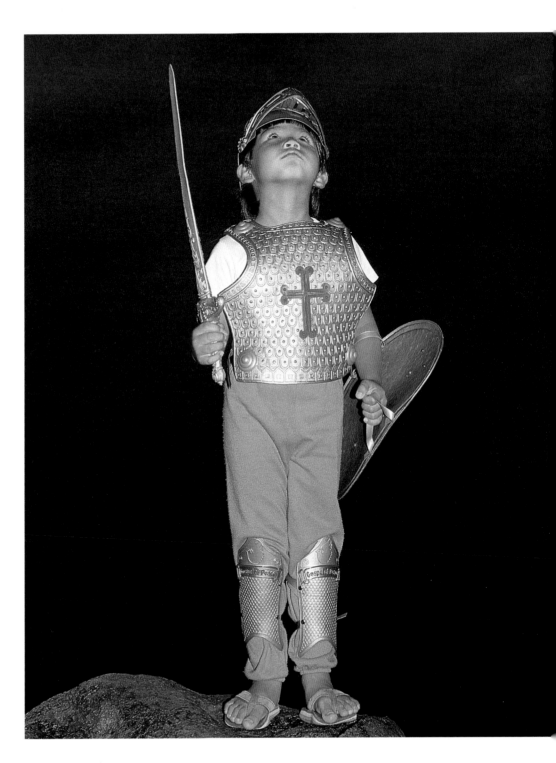

◀

Celebrating New Year's island style

▶

Doing something special is going to
birthday parties.

Spending a day at the Zoo

Being in a Christmas play is
   very special

So is getting cotton candy at a carnival

Or playing in the School Band

Being in — or watching — Kamehameha
Day and Aloha Week parades is
extra special

◀

I like to be a hula dancer in Maui for
    my auntie.
She likes us to dance for her in Maui.
I like to dance for anybody, like on
    birthdays,
babies' first birthday parties
and anniversaries and weddings.

▶

When I dance hula
I feel special.

Every summer, Bon Odori is a special
time of remembering with joy.
In Kona
Everyone
Dances
All night.

Graduation is a special end and the
special beginning
of a new phase of life.